There is This

Also by Toni Thomas:

Chosen	Brick Road Poetry Press
Fast as Lightening	Gribble Press
Walking on Water	Finishing Line Press
Blue Halo	Annalese Press
Ace Raider of the Unfathomable Universe	Annalese Press
You'll be Fast as Lightning Coveting my Painted Tail	Annalese Press
Hotsy Totsy Ballroom	Annalese Press
Love Adrift in the City of Stars	Annalese Press
In the Pink Arms of the City	Annalese Press
In the Kingdom of Longing	Annalese Press
The Things We Don't Know	Annalese Press
In the Boarding House for Unclaimed Girls	Annalese Press
They Became Wing Perfect and Flew	Annalese Press
Unburdened Kisses	Annalese Press
Bandits Come and Remove Her Body in the Night	Annalese Press
Here	Annalese Press

There is This

Poems

First published in 2023 by Annalese Press
134 Towngate
Netherthong
Holmfirth
West Yorkshire HD9 3XZ
England

Copyright © 2001 Toni Thomas

Please Note
All characters and situations appearing
in these pages are in the service of poetry.
Any resemblance to real persons,
living or dead, is purely coincidental.

All rights reserved. No part of this publication
may be reproduced, stored, or transmitted in any
form, or by any means electronic, mechanical or
photocopying, recording or otherwise, without the
express written permission of the publisher.

Photograph by Peter Wadsworth
Cover design and layout by Peter Wadsworth
Painting *Mother and Child* by Julius Gari Melchers
Circa 1906, Art Institute Chicago

British Library Cataloguing-in-Publication Data
A catalogue record for this book is available on
request from the British Library.

ISBN 978-1-9163620-9-3

Acknowledgements

Appreciation goes to the following publications-

"Winter Solstice" *Cold Mountain Review*
"Burnt Offerings" *Obsessed with Pipework* (England)
"Waking Dreams" *Takahe* (New Zealand)

Contents

Prologue

Waking Dreams   3

Part One

This Key We Enter By   7
Winter Solstice   9
Possession   10
Black with Gold Borders   13
That Hand-Hold Knot Still Dangles   15

Part Two

Glass Milk Jars Rattling   21
The Red Flowering Currents   23
There is This   25
Recomposing the Mosaic   28
Holy Week   30

Part Three

Burnt Offerings   35
The Silent Beehives   36
Rattling the Shingles Loose   37
To the Unborn One Growing Iris   39
Promises   42

Part Four

Snowfields   49
New Born   50
Yellow Satin   51
Floating Down a Mountain Stream   53
Sandstone   55
The Offering   56

Queen rose of the rosebud garden of girls,
Come hither, the dances are done,
In gloss of satin and glimmer of pearls,
Queen lily and rose in one;
Shine out, little head, sunning over with curls,
To the flowers, and be their sun.
Queen rose of the rosebud garden of girls,
Come hither, the dances are done,
In gloss of satin and glimmer of pearls,
Queen lily and rose in one;
Shine out, little head, sunning over with curls,
To the flowers, and be their sun.

      from *Maude,* Alfred Lord Tennyson

PROLOGUE

Waking Dreams

I'm waiting for the world to bend into children
who trace themselves with available light.

It is dawn, cold, and I am not at home
my sleep in this stranger's bed a schism
between something once known and
the uneasy middle aged body I might become.

Not all things become themselves
not all of us walk on water
get hoisted onto durable shoulders.
But I am getting ahead of myself
like the small germ of faith you turn in my hand
hamsters that bumble my dreams
all those who no longer philander through
midnight gardens of drunken roses.

You unbraid my hair early
your bracelet a slim curve of loss
in the shadow of my face.
Slow I reach for your mandolin nightshirt
milky pearls, shy cousins
that slumber open in our rarest bed.

The morning returns on bent knee.
Kisses travel my hair
spend themselves up and down
till I am a journey of goose bumps
satin morning slippers
the child's open purse lent whole cloth
to see me into this day.

PART ONE

This Key We Enter By

For years I came to the kitchen of comfort
to lick my wounds
pulled down canisters of flour, sugar
sure they would see me through another trip
into the trials of the forgotten
the blue boxes of childhood
where my fragile headed porcelain dolls
waited for the orange hour of play.

And mother of wild auburn hair, loose cotton
I searched for you there
away from the tie tacks, creased trousers
tall buildings that housed tall men
shaven faces
away from school walls chalked
with the faint graffiti
of forlorn boys.

But always you were elsewhere.
The mixing bowls, supper plates, ironed shirts
never could hold you
not even the stretched arms
of the open window
let in enough Spring air, sunshine
to keep you inside
waiting for me.

Again and again
I came to the kitchen of comfort
licked my wounds
folded my fear into the pure smooth
white of cake batter.
And I remember your shadowy silhouette
tucked away in the hours
of moon and cricket cried madness
after the last want

had been folded into the bureau
after you painted all the walls black
only then did you appear
lips alternating between ice cream
the puff of your drawn-out cigarettes.

My chain of beads hangs
limp like a sunken rosary
sparkles only now and again
hangs in the apple orchard
high meadow
beside the bank of the river
on the hackneyed trail etched by deer
that ride quiet, imperceptible
up the north rump of Saddle Mountain.

Back there
in the small house of four walls
is a kitchen
place of heaven or hell
depending on which key you enter by.
Tonight a frog anthems
its quarter moon sonata.
The black spaniel and I sit on the porch
listen.
Inside the cat begs for food
my tablecloth needs mending.
Almost two quarters of a century
of my life gone to the floorboards
like a junco feather scribbled
away in the wind.
I can't go back there anymore.

Winter Solstice

Come winter heavy footed fishermen
hammer board, erect steel drums
saw circles in the ice of the pond
where lines will drop down
tempt bass, pickerel.

And what happens if the ice cracks
one of the men slips into frigid water
dark as sin
scrambles to take hold
what happens if luck drags
he is unable to drink the return
travel back with something precious
unspeakable?

George Kirby will not come back.
Two years ago, after the first heavy snow
the winter pond claimed him.
His headstone rests up the hill
at the cemetery in Wakefield.

This January the men will return
once the ice sets, drill their holes
erect huts, stoke a flame
huddle around with cigarettes, coffee
talk of politics, religion
the shit hunting season, rifles.

A few have laid a 5 or 10 dollar bill down
for the chance of Winner's Circle
their bodies bent low, watchful.
Day after day they tough it out
armed with the resolve of Job
to bag that one illusive prize.

Possession

When I sat on the hillside in Capernaum
the sky an untroubled blue, fig trees, cicadas
untangling their songs amid the swollen branches
I was young, my hair loose in the lilt of breezes
decked in cut-offs, the sandals of the unknowing ones
who breath beneath unabridged juntas
where angels hover to polish their wings
in the sun's blind benevolence.

When I was 26 I recrossed the sea
on the wings of a jetliner
went back to Capernaum
saw my feet wrapped in the canvas rags
of a China woman, I saw the gates of Janus
sunken down, drowned in time like the lost city
of Atlantis, and I saw how the wrath of Zeus
had blown the angels into hiding, and I traveled
the path of the scattered seeds, and I sat beneath
the wall of wailing in the city of Jerusalem
and I saw the Sea of Galilee peopled with speedboats
towlines skimming the surface, saw the shelled windows
vacant villages locked behind barbed wire
saw men in uniforms hug rifles along the Gaza Strip
and I watched the people of the early dawn ascend
the coiled path to the ruins of Jericho
while the valley floor below hummed with bees
and bougainvillea, effused green in the center of dry rock
and I saw the vapor trail rising from the skin
of the Dead Sea, dipped inside till my arms became flame
and I ran for cover, hid inside the fancy hotel
with the air conditioning, iced cokes.

When I went down the path behind the farmhouse
yesterday afternoon, 38 years old and young
this journey flecked with minefields, the shallow
pools shy of minnows beckoning, eager to make my way

before the sun's banishment, down past the old rusted
farm machinery, the thresher, clumps of scotch broom
invading the meadow, this undergrowth of thick fern
tangled vines that want to bury my feet, not let go
this carpet of green moss spread indiscriminately
about me on the forest floor
I came to the manger, once home of goats, sheep
empty now with the hay soft, dry, a waiting bed
solid place where our Christmas tree was laid to rest
slow disintegration on her way back to Elysium.
I came here and I sat
sat on the crumbled walls of Jericho
drank the vile of the Dead Sea
sat till once again I was on the hillside at Capernaum
till this was a new place, buoyant like a cloud lifting.
The gnarled apple boughs, slumped pines had grown back
and by the pond we pump for bath water
where the skunk cabbage sprout yellow corn cobs
in the center of their leaves
… there she was—one angel
oiling her wings in the sun's cloud banked disguise.

And I said *Perhaps I cannot turn back.*
I have changed, the road long clotted with dust
disuse, the stretched skin of the graying citadels
shoes laced too tight.
I have sunk in the river of the seven virgins
know the rasp of tarantulas biting at my heels
know the uneasy rhetoric reverberating off
the mahogany wall of the prison cells, know the blood
of my mothers rattling their bones beneath
smooth stones.

And the wind came up suddenly from nowhere
grabbed my words, swept them into a burlap sack studded
with cow manure, stirred them the way my grandmother

stirred her sorrel soup till the broth thickened
and the marsh hawk alone
dying circles of hunger above the pasture
pecked inside the sack, nibbled my words like ebony prayers
finally spit the remains back till the words reverberated
inside the air as song and only then
did the angel's face rise to meet them.
She nodded, at me and at no one
went back to oiling her wings
as if the pillars of Janus were this manger
as if the sun shone clear, clear as a bell
just as when I was a child in Capernaum
as if nothing was hidden behind the cloud cover.

And I sat longer
watched fish sprout along the limbs of the maple
watched the sheen of the fish bellies
embossed with colored sequins sewn
by the brown hands of Guatemalan women
and I sat longer, watched while
the angel continued preening her wings, preened them
as only the self-possessed know how to do.

Black With Gold Borders

Over the years you filed your teeth with an emery board
till they grew fence posts.
I didn't like it, wanted to open the gate
pull the girl-child inside the woman close to me
say *it's all right*
but you departed, too soon this dying away
before what could be born unspooled.
Heart failure, gone in a flash, the same flash
the neutron bomb makes when it freezes skin
to dry wall, turns a grown boy back into bone.

I witnessed the fire of your art
how it drowned in the bathwater
crept into the beaks of flamingos
folded into my stained white shirts
remember the swish of your paintbrush
our walls, ceilings turned black
in the loosened sleeves of the night
between the puff of your cigarettes.

As your blue eyes sank into the low C
of those violin strings, you stitched
that crystal rosary, bead after bead
into the seam of my dressing gown
hoped like a lost dove it would nest
find a home.

The fact is—he never understood you
for years you sprinkled cool water
on my father's bleeding forehead, deflected
the wrath of his words till finally they crept
inside your own mouth, a bundle of rocks
that would not let go.

It's hot today.
I carry your worn wishes like mango

dark serpents I can't dislodge.
There was no one to save me back then
so I built a tent in my imagination
climbed inside.
I could not save you.
Later I ran off to England and saved myself.

Maybe I'll never understand this fire that flailed
was doused back down by the stout arms of the fathers
the love that clung between you made of barren wafer
the rodeo rider you ran off with at twenty
before the forced annulment and the solid shadow
of my father appeared, before you were roped back
in by the prudence of German elders
before your low cut satin gowns, riding boots, easels
were tucked away in cargo trunks
to gather dust in the basement.
Dust I later scribbled my name in.
Maybe I'll never understand
never get to hold you in my arms
get beyond the sea walls that eventually divided us.

You sent me off with broken wings
and still I take you with me, watch your ashes float
flocks of geese on the forearms of the sea
smell the lemon mixed with henna
in the strands of your pageboy
watch you hoist the sails—barefoot
bare chested, your body at last
a gleam of silver fish, blazing sun.

That Hand-Hold Knot Still Dangles

Someone once told me that cement shoes
anchor the soul in place, and the cemetery
up in the alder grove behind Wakefield village
holds the charred remains of a woman burned
at the stake 123 years ago when the church drank
white sheets off the farmers' clotheslines
tied a knot of renunciation around would-be heathens.

Of course, I'm not sure I believe any of this
all hearsay, I suspect, like the story of Joe McKay
the only pipefitter in town, married with seven kids
who drove his pickup up toward Ossipee
to hunt bear one October, never came back.
Sister Rosemary of the Immaculate Conception School
swears she saw him two seasons later on her only jubilee
trip to the Holy Land, dressed in poor sandals
a dirt speckled robe kneeling beside the base
of the Wailing Wall.
Not even Mrs. McKay, or six of the seven children
believed that one.

The town holds its silence like a dented tin cup
only in summer and fall do the streets buzz
with the tourists from Boston. They stay up the hill
where the views are good, tucked away
in the freshly scrubbed farmhouses with
wraparound porches, wooden rockers.
The swimming hole west of town remains unposted
place where kids skittle off, discharge their squeals
squirting limbs, stop asking *what for?, how come?*

These days the disused railroad station has been
reclaimed as a preschool.
The steam trains that rode past Sanborneville
up to Wolfboro on the lake and back have vanished
an early cemetery some say

and one old train enthusiast's dream
gone to ember
beside the weed stricken tracks.

I come here to buy milk, bread, write
grab toast and eggs in the local breakfast joint
watch the teenage waitresses
fresh faced, tanned in their cutoffs
complain about how little there is to do
while a couple of old-timers at the counter
finger the obituaries
check the fishing report to see what's biting.
The girls' eyes say they will run away to big cities
neon lights, the pull of well-paying jobs
reliable men.

I drink my coffee, prick the last yellow head
of egg on my plate, know the long rope with
the hand-hold knot two thirds down still dangles
off that huge sulky maple that sits with her mangled roots
half over the edge of the embankment, dips her toes
ungangly in the swimming hole up past Fossil Road
and I know the cemetery hasn't changed much
a couple of dozen or so graves, the small headstones
polished and rimmed in fresh pansies, plastic daisies.
Today, old Mrs. Grimpbell will tend the shelves
arrange for the Saturday bake sale at the one room library.
They need the cash.
And Hank, the butcher, with 20 years under his belt
at the Piggly Wiggly Market, has reason to sweat beneath
his blood stippled hands now that half the patrons have
exiled allegiance, won over by the blue and white
bargain flyers that come straight to their door
from the new supermarket mall up on Highway 16.

I finish my coffee, watch the kids through the window
balance their tins of worms, cheap fishing rods
as they bike over toward Pine River Creek.

And I wonder over our times, this place of
trilling frog ponds, odd jobs, sunken pockets
wonder about the weight or sheer lightness
of cement shoes
those rusted, blood-red clotheslines.

PART TWO

Glass Milk Jars Rattling

Tonight your words sit on my tongue
black licorice, no sacramental host.
Back in my father's house
a girl child cowers under the weight of his scale
shuttle her porcelain dolls into their blue boxes.
Rain rips the clear morning sky to shreds.

There now, and she prays the prayer of the initiated
glides a comb through each doll's hair
soothes their tiny foreheads with a damp cloth
just as I imagine the mothers do, tenderly stroke
the fevered one till he swallows the dark bread
comes back.

Tonight the room is mercurial
fire of passion turns the initiated song into ember.
Part of me longs to take your axe handles
rosewater and quinine vows
hurl them till they puncture the cast iron stove
into a fountain of water holes.
The other part longs to pick you up in my easy arms
spin you slowly, gentle under the spreading light

there now, to find again the God
inside the man inside the boy
whose mouth turned to stone.
There now ssshhh, and rub and rub
the spleen of your back till fire-eating dragons recant
your gray head turns birdsong again.

One day the woman won't run from the woods
your furled brow
hide and write at the Dairy Queen.
The dolls will no longer shiver in their blue
metal boxes. They'll emerge, one by one, slowly

each in her good time, anxious to sip juice, suck mango
lounge in the stories of dark skinned women
offering up red invitation under the magnolia tree.

And finally, the girl with the missing
two front teeth who dripped red spaghetti sauce
down her white first communion dress
when she tried to eat like the grownups
in the shadow of their shirttails
will dislodge the pebbles
you placed in her mouth of clay.

The Red Flowering Currents

I want to offer you more than the swell
of the food's nuptial set in the cower
of your mother's strict china
the lilt of modest breezes that never ruffle
nor flood the stacks of computer pages
that herald a desk.

You are asleep in the eaves.
Night beckons the once head banging
child who rattled the bars of his crib into oblivion.
Come with me. Softly, very softly.
I cup your hands in the wings of feather doves.
You alight from your bed.
It is frightening to be free.
Periwinkle chiffon roams the night air
anthem of frogs, coyote, buttercups
hiding their fiery faces in the tall grass.

Above us in the heavens, ethereal
round bosomed and beckoning
the seven sisters reach down
untie the knot of your ponytail
pull the pins one by one from the high crown
of my head, till our hair is a feather duster
for the floating sails of chiffon and on
the quarterdeck an obstreperous moon nudges
the others to be still—*watch, watch.*

I untie the crimson shawl from my breast
wrap it around and around you, a loose cradle
in the whirling dervish of the dark.
They, who know we are mere novitiates, watch us.
The wind lifts, the red flowering currents
a forked flame shimmering their bosoms

like buttons popping open on a woman's
fine satin bodice.

The oat field welcomes us
the ebb and flow of our bodies
fevered brow.
In the morning you will search your desk
the stacks of computer pages
insure nothing is missing.
The pearl buttons will slip back
through the holes of my white blouse
and the chiffon, the quarterdeck will slide
down into deeper realms
taunt us to reinvent them again and again.

There Is This

The midwife tells me I'm going to be a mother
Get used to it she says.
I watch the Mexican girls come into the clinic
shepherded by relations, so young
their long braids of shiny black hair
colored cottons, prospect of migrant camps
strawberry fields, fate easily accepted
with each Hail Mary, sign of the cross
that swings across the gleaming gold
of their neck chains.

I am almost 40, have had a hard time growing up
in an age of grownups, knew even back then
the five Our Father's and four Hail Mary's
the priest gave me in the confessional
would not save me from sin's nuptial
don't know how to diaper, burp a newborn
bathe a tiny body under the garden sprinkler.
The black spaniel who waits Buddha patience
for me in the driveway, his greeting
all licks and wagging tail like a youngster
who cannot contain his joy at the very being
of this moment in this very world
will be jealous at first, uneasy to share his night
vigil at our bed with anyone else.

I do not tell you—*you're going to be a father
get used to it* or that life has a masterful way
of upsetting even our finest laid dinner hour
in the name of what we've yet to know.
I tell you little, watch you squirm and fret
finger the blank pages that mark the third section
of your novel, the interruptions you cannot bear
life's inconveniences dampening your *necessary*
solitude in the woods.

And I know the Santos, carved in wood by the hands of
the Guatemalan women, my gift to you on Christmas
is the real culprit behind this.
Your lips resist this miracle of new life
till only a tough rind remains.

This April I have planted an exceptional flower garden
nasturtiums, Gerber daisies, dahlias, iris, lobelia, cosmos
profusion of roses, sunflower stalks, borders of onion.
Inside me, a baby turns arms, legs, rolls tiny shoulders
till my stomach seems to be a sea swell of expectancy.
Already, I am sure this child will adore flowers.

And I tell you—*You drive me crazy*
and one morning I threw a pitcher of water
on your head to cool down the ticking
and *no* I'm not here to rescue you
nor crush my own spirit in the name of sainthood.
And silly, strange, and solitary man that you are
perhaps I know you better than the rest
know the storms you tend of your own making
see the pained lonely boy inside the man
the disdain for failure your parents drove in
fear of love, prison walls that can latch the heart.
And I know too how the hummingbirds gather faithfully
for the sugar water of your feeder
and I know your tender fingers, how they nurse
the yellowed tomato plants back
encourage the pole beans, chard, pea vines to shoot up
just you, the frogs, the crickets out in the field
mouthing Rilke.

And beneath everything *there is this*—
unexplainable, naive perhaps
dismissed as delusional idealism by some cynics
by others proclaimed the elixir of life—

however you name it
this faith I live by
know I don't give up on love easily
nor on difficult strange men
who live the whole burden of art in their bones

nor the promise of new life that always rasps
at our doorway—crazy, unpredictable burden that it is
arrives holding a bouquet of field daisies
fairy slippers
dressed to kill
waits patient for us to turn the key.

Recomposing The Mosaic

It is the fourth Sunday of Lent.
I've given up nothing—perhaps for my pride
and what the avenue bearing the initial of
Christ into the new world would look like
I don't know.

Everywhere I feel the ripeness of spring
like a woman's breasts swelling slow
to welcome the suck of a newborn's lips.
Purple and lemon crocus, trumpets of daffodils
three pointed trillium on the hill
fans of iris inch up through dark earth.
And I wonder at my own obstinance
years of pounding pavement that led to nothing
except fractured eggs, lament.

This summer I will be 40.
Two thirds of a life spent in learning how to live
my hands trying to shape the dough
into loaves that would sustain, rise full
not fall inside the center of the oven
bread fit to break into wedges for the guests
at the dinner table I have yet to know.

I eat alone.
What have I to offer this child inside my womb
swelling in the unease of my own body?
I play the flute badly, the xylophone keys shiver
in want beneath their coat of dust.
What have I to offer the gods in this time
of weeping and childhood madness gone
to the wall of our uneasy indentures?

Outside the raspberries need pruning
weeds have overtaken the new growth at the root.
With my whole life filled with split seams, yellow taffeta

I go out to walk this field with the black dog.
We have come too far to turn back now
on the heels of distemper.

The ceramic angel on the chimney ledge fell off
the night before the abortion date I could not keep
broke into twelve pieces across the top of the parlor stove.
We glued her back slow, piece by piece
till the wings and head became a mosaic of sorts
a chipped edge, newly composed beauty.

The grapevines up the dirt road by the Strassel farm
will not be ready to harvest till September, yet already
this flourishing of delicate pink skinned blossoms
the knobby trees in the apple orchard a swell of new buds
this hope I cling to in the midst of rain.

Holy Week

Vermillion. Yes. That's what she wore
splashed like a painter's brush across
the careless weave of her days.
I wanted her, wanted to wrestle
the tiger of her muscled forelegs, send shivers
up and down her spine, wrestle her
into oblivion like the mother who
wrestled me to the floor
bleeding in my tracks—a broken boy
banging his head on the crib spindles.
No one came.

I wanted her like the choirboy
searching a madonna of perfect pitch
white, sanctimonious, yielding her veil
lightly lightly for the graze of my cheeks
her lips soft, fluid as peaches
that never bruise, turn rancid.

Vermillion. Yes. That's what she wore.
A temptress, tarantula. Not to be trusted
like Eve with her apple riddled with the worms
of disharmony's season. Lips, legs dripping
with what was yet to be born.

Holy Week. The two Marys there
at death's burial. Myrrh, frankincense
oil of almonds to rub my body in
after the cross's annunciation.

No. Not you. The other, the other.
They both stepped forward.
I am afraid
to lay down
to lay open.
They anoint me with oil.

Lay me in fine white linen.
In the garden of Gethsemane
blood red magnolia trees, bougainvillea.
Lay me to rest, for Christ's sake.

PART THREE

Burnt Offerings

You, the querying fiction writer, point to a poem in *Harpers*
ask me what's the difference between this and
what they call *prose* these days.
I read the line about a supermarket
woman rising above the highway
fish and chip vendor gone to desertion
and I have no sophistry to lay at your door.

I tell you about the man who took a sudden leap
off the Golden Gate Bridge when no one was looking
how the fish might have been a gold mirror
feeding up at the surface of the half moon.
Perhaps they were the lure, like some lost virgin
who came into his life on the tailgate of a youthful summer
disappeared when the harvest grew bare
perhaps he saw gold coins of fish scales or his own image
mirrored back across the silver sheen of the lit water
and at last dove in to meet it.
Perhaps his life made no difference, perhaps no one was
waiting back at the apartment pacing the floorboards to ruin
at the lateness of the hour, perhaps his vacancy left a hole
no one can fill, or a hole already had broken open
that longed to be filled once and for all at midnight
in January under a half moon.

All I know is that tonight I sit here, look at you
my tongue a burnt offering of unctuous answers
that slip inside fountain pens, that on January 22, 1994
under the eaves of a third quarter moon
between the Golden Gate Bridge and Alcatraz
a big flock of mirrors were floating.

The Silent Beehives

When the night rests in the stirrups of the moon and
the virgin bends her back, tips the Big Dipper earthward
how many times have I stalked, blind Sisyphus rolling
the rock up the hill while the stones in the meadow
glistened with the dew of sky water?

No one comes in the cuff of my call.
The black turd piles in the bedded grass of the coyote
tell me he too has been stalking this meadow
hunger has never been bound to the rites of the human body
and his howl clips the raw air like a tooth mark—
jagged, thirsting out there somewhere in the oat field
beyond the telegraph shack.

How many nights have I raised the red ember of my cigarette
up toward the constellations, afraid to give in
to crumble back to earth and howl the last screech
of the coyote, to spread-eagle across the dirt
till my body is coated in the slime of elders buried long ago
and long forgotten, the same dirt I will one day be buried in
dead carcass of one human fool—buried dead or alive—
we have our choices.

Tonight the virgin is unruly, blows puffballs
across the western sky. I am tired of running away
tired of the rouged embers that fan my heart.
The crickets, the myrtle are pulsing.
The hollow bellied coyote has slipped off elsewhere.
How many times have I yearned to hold your chalice
up to the night wind, the clotted stars
cup the sky water of the silent beehives?

A voice says—*Give in. For god's sake, let go!*
And the red ember dies across the Pleiades.
Ordinary rainwater rips my fallen face into ribbon.

Rattling the Shingles Loose

The wind howls today
and an anguished mother drowns
in the vacant bed of her stolen kisses.
On the porch obsidian chimes dangle
collide into psalm.

I am in bed
my father's down comforter tucked up to my chin
listen to the storm windows shimmy, shingles quiver
insistent as a child who rattles the same invocation
hands wooing other hands
but nobody comes.

The radio predicts wind of sixty, seventy miles per hour.
I imagine the waves on the coast, their swell
high as your breasts rising
the delicate sand dollars, fluted scallop shells
swept clean from their shelves of tide
bodies shifting everywhere
from Gold Beach north to Tillamook.

Heavy footsteps climb the stairs
a cup of tea arrives
and you say in your faithless voice -
The power is gone. No lights anywhere.
My day rethinks itself, I hear the child rattling
peel myself slowly out of the covers
descend the farmhouse stairs long after your vanishing.
Back in the kitchen reinvent your face
all shine and boy softness in the glow of two candles
watch your body in its brow of silence
bent over the dragon china

watch your mouth accept from your hand
one solid spoonful of porridge at a time.

It's true—the power is gone, electric shortage
they say on the connecting lines.
A child's hand shakes the rattle in fits
and starts, sound of the many beaded rosary
blue crystal that the old woman fingered once
at my altar of childhood, rosary that dropped
inside the pond of tears
waited to turn gold.

To the Unborn One Growing Iris

If I could offer you that flame of orange
at the neck of our hummingbirds
dress you in the bold trumpets that reach
unabashed at the center of daffodils
if I knew the words, the whispers inside a world
of subtle fluted innocence, bells that never crack
under the fierceness of hands angry for what
cannot be lived
I would give you all this, and more.

The light would rise gentle over your forehead
and the worn dolls in the blue metal boxes
I have kept for you would hover round
when the pain of this world grew too tight
and your blue eyes yearned to go back
to the dark warmth of those eternal fetal waters
moon soaked nights.

But what have I to offer you, child growing inside me
what gem can I set before you
when you finally emerge, your pink body wrinkled
drenched in fluid and blood from the uneasy place
of my own being?

Where the bells, the jonquils
ladders of purple iris
happy nursery swaying in calico
where will the father be who can welcome you
all open arms and blessed invitation?
You come on the wings of a ragged age
a time of trials and fallen backs
shaven countenances.
In a month I must move.

I do not know what inn may have room
for our guest slippers

understand a world where gold coins, callow words
love gone impatient
gain passage to the windowless temples.

Our temple, little one, must be different from this.
That goat manger down past the spring in the woods
perhaps this is your birthright
and unawares women I don't know
will come, bring you fruit, a basket of nosegays.

And what have I to make me worthy of motherhood?
Half spent reams of poems cluster around windows
my body an accordion, lost in its ability to expand graceful
those red sashes, crisp white bodices hang limp
wrinkled, shudder furious in the closet of wanton laments.

The black spaniel follows us gaily up and down
the hills, oblivious to the scotch broom
the prickly blackberry vines that nail my legs
won't let go.
Late afternoon I plant an old corrugated window box
two small barrels. Fill with bedding plants
renuncula, gerber daisies the color of salamanders.
Carefully I separate the roots, stretch as far as I can
the economy of my three garden trays.

You will need to be patient. The smaller starts
will not take hold and flower for a while yet.
Like you this slow, tenuous growth
under the precarious life-giving milk of April.
Wherever we move, how little, how much, we will have this
a flower garden for you who deserves so much more
than I can give and who must make dew
with the drawn circles of the moon

flutter of saved trees whispering your unknown name
within the cemetery of the dead.

If you are ordained—it is to life
not to me, I am but the fumbling Magdalene
at the tomb, dumbfounded and dazed
clutching my half spent pitcher
small pocket of oil to give.

Promises

I don't want to talk about the man
who whittled away up the road
on a trail swamped in maidenfern
lupine hanging on in the postmortem of
an Oregon heatwave, the way the old
Ford pickup could be forgiven for blocking the trail
the way its bed held a man's body like a broken chalice
the pact with death consecrated on forsaken knees.

For three days, three nights he laid there
the flies, mosquitoes, heavy dew unable to disrupt
the pink fleshiness of his skin
disrupt that grace that comes once the battle
with weeping angels has been won.
An empty beer can, crushed milk carton
wads of white tissue strewn across low branches
like Christmas tree garland - the silent eulogy
that remains to consecrate a motionless Christ
unable to resurrect himself till the squad cars
finally arrive at the end of the third day.
How he was hoisted onto a stretcher of white linen
his truck was hoisted too, all in less than two hours.
Almost nothing remains.

I haven't wanted to talk about the man
who stumbled from his life on broken wings
how one after another of his childhood mouths
his lovers, his sorrows, stole away.
And I want to forget the way my mother
departed her life, all silent shivers
an absent shawl, the misdiagnosis
sudden early a.m. collapse
death by cardiac arrest, three days

into the New Year and 3,000 miles away.
The mother who will never see her only grandchild
a satisfied life, a man whose hands and lips
know how to tender.

Losses. How do I count them?
My mother and father, their love gone stale.
The black spaniel with Buddha patience
who pants heavy into the wool of our living room carpet
knows a trust, loyalty I can only guess at
as he tumbles away from my arms and toward death.
Two weeks ago forty acres of Douglas fir
toppled just beyond the lip of the sheep meadow.
The woods, quarry loop trail, small pathways
that deer and elk pass over gone now
to accommodate a thirsting world.
A wide angle view of the coast range
barnyard of stumps asks to substitute
where a forest once breathed.

I want to tell you that death hurts like a million bee stings
my mother wanted her casket closed so we wouldn't
witness the unsung lines of her face
would succor the living instead of the dead.
I want to say death hurts
even when it's a strange man you don't know
in a pickup off a dirt road.

I may never understand these losses
that haunt my leanest hours, the way pain
loneliness slays the voice, drives in a silent stake
or festers for years till it erupts
a heart splintered in unpastable pieces.
I may never understand how my black spaniel

manages to stumble through his days
the love that still arrives to comfort me on periled wings
how the flora and fauna of this earth
ourselves, our lives can be cast away in unredeemable pieces
or the way my mother's anger carries invisible seeds
all those diminishing men, all the ashes
she wanted sent out to sea along with her own.

PART FOUR

Snowfields

Maybe life was always meant
to be understood like this
a miracle waiting to happen.
Small girls availing themselves
of material light
flowers that burst forth unnoticed
indigo in the unclaimed woods.
Your feet are poised between love
and the backdoor
jocular cousins that wear thin
slippers to bare bone.

Maybe life was always meant
to be a tumble in cardboard boxes
down broken hills
snow so deep you can marry yourself
when no one is looking.

You have frost on your breath
eyes as blue and big as the marbles
you invite for your games of play.
I want to wrap you in cashmere
an ancient mariner's map.
You have frost on your breath
tarry in snowfields
the miracle
already
blinking
to begin.

New Born

Simple table.
Laid out with your lament.
Borders of red berries
rise in clusters
move past their own weeping
and into the snow.

I might never come back here
touch these faces that love conquers
without a word
hold the willows
wing of bird
dilapidation of paradise
in my hands

this new child
who calls to me
out of the rain.

Yellow Satin

And I remember how we made love
in the Japanese Garden
under the wood beams of the sun shelter
rattan mats swaying against the arms of the side joists
how I slipped my sandals off
raised myself on tiptoe
to meet the smooth curve of your chin
lips so beckoning that desire was an anagram
to the stars and we were her infidels
how on that day we courted her, the one
who began and never came, a fallen kiss
in the cleaving ax of your reasonable expletives
eleven weeks later, after the stones I turned
round and round in my sweated palms
she was gone, aborted
unaware of yellow satin, too soon this dying
away of what was yet to be born.

The yellow sundress hangs, a sad virgin
wrapped in clear plastic, sealed, inconsolable.
You no longer spin yellow ribbon between your fingers
no longer hear the subtle wind wash through
the magnolia till they are a splay of fire
splashed jagged across slate tiles
and the *drip drip drip* of the water
like some torture treatment
I've heard will break down the will
of any stubborn-minded man or woman
has not melted you.

Ponds are everywhere in the Japanese Garden
and drips from the hollow center of long bamboo reeds
move slow, sure into the waiting pools, into
the mouths of giant goldfish who know the secret
of our transgression—three years ago and *she*
a memory of the risen mouthed blossom

and yes how their shiny orange scales are bristling
to see me here, alone—the return—
with a seven month old boy child on my back
bristling to see how I watch your absent faces
in the pool of glass.

Floating Down A Mountain Stream

Last night the moon offered herself
in the Aquarian sky, ran off to meet
the seven sisters when her lover did not come.
Today, thimbleberries bright as red buttons
on a child's rain slicker pop off their stems
to meet the red blood of your mouth peopled with
seeds.

Perhaps I feared the moon could not hold you
all full faced, bosomy on the night you broke
the waters of the underworld, floated
along the passageway of that clear mountain
stream, puddled down my legs
into my arms.

How slow, delicate you offered yourself
to this very world.
And perhaps the child in the rain slicker
will not forget the ladder that climbs
the cherry orchard to the sun.
No matter. The path of stones steams
like the bright embers of an autumn heat wave.
Your feet have practiced the calluses
of so many knuckled roadways
passed the stunned amber snakes sunning themselves
on the rocks before afternoon vespers.
You have come this far - bow of the celestial archer
steady of heart, the fine strands of silk
unweaving themselves before me one by one.
The loons call to you with each dying breath

and the black spaniel, loyal as a monk
will not leave your side.

My child friend, don't turn back now.
There is a clearing some know by dusk
others in the watery shadow of the slippery moon.
It calls *enter enter enter*.
We stumble, fall in
a stupor of drunken love song.

Sandstone

I don't know my way around this thing
like the fevered *no* in our lovemaking that proceeds the *yes*
how my mother made her way to the grave in hurried fists
those spiny dark rattles unyielding in the space between nice
the black spaniel who walks his way out of my life
like a cancerous Buddha exiled from beneath the Bo tree.

Maybe we make a covenant of sorts
the way quartz stones hold to the earth
in a fluid act of devotion
the way my child's lips cling steadfastly
to the balm of breast
maybe there is no left or right
and the face we scrubbed yesterday, painstakingly
will take us into another day and another
steadfast on pleated knees.
Maybe I will never know my way around this thing
the weight of loss that haunts my meanest hours
the face of the father rubbed soft as sandstone.

Maybe we make a covenant of sorts
the Buddha dog panting his way serenely toward death
my child who looks on, unaccustomed to losses, insistent
on the sanctity of this very moment, the surety
as he fields the way into first words
once the silent ones are safely laid
to bless.

The Offering

You re-enter the Japanese Gardens
filled with birdseed, an alluvium sunset
the million nights we ran from each other
ran from ourselves.
No perfect propositions
the yellow sundress still a covenant
I long to enter
your hands across my body sure
as the pool that welcomes us back
translucent fish
some steadfast allegiance to home.

Autumn.
Ordinary shoes retrace ancient footsteps
linger the remains of the day's glory.
Maple leaves rise, flame to death mid-air.
My child dreams chocolate, a red sleigh
snow so deep we can bury ourselves.

Your gum boots collide with my fake leopard muff
resurrected from a childhood grave
the breath of angels titillates
long as icicles hymned along the rim of a wedding cake.
Gold rings placed on our fingers
filial, round as the circle dances young girls make
who have woven suffering into their stones
rings without end, sure as the first glance we gave
across the length of a cafe table
the liquid blue eyes of infinity
caught in our faltering nets.

See those exotic islands of nuptial bliss
how they float or sink at the torch of a matchstick

Gauguin's voluptuous bodies blessed and stained
with the mock indigo caress of gardenias
mortal wounds.

You sprinkle pomegranate seeds over our heads
slit open mango
drown us in juice, scarlet seedbeds
as if the world might end tomorrow
as if the garden path always leads here
the open, pared down bed
twine of leaves and moss
the moon lisping
this tragic world
miraculous garden we tender.

Toni Thomas lives in Portland, Oregon. Her poems have been published in Austria, Spain, New Zealand, Canada, England, Scotland, and Australia. In the United States her work has appeared in over fifty literary magazines including *Prairie Schooner, North Dakota Quarterly, Hayden's Ferry Review, the Minnesota Review, Notre Dame Review, Poetry East*, and more. She has been twice nominated for a Pushcart prize, and won several awards. She has published sixteen collections of poetry and four books for children.

Her figurative clay sculptures have been shown in gallery exhibits in Portland and Chicago, displayed in literary magazines, and housed in private collections in the U.S. and England.

Her short documentary *One of Us* was shown at the Trans-ideology: Nostalgia festival in Berlin and at the Museum of Contemporary Art in Taipei.

Since Toni loves to create and sits buried in reams of poems, manuscripts, clay figures and images….she likes to imagine all of them out in the world, swaying wild as the lupine.

tonithomaspoetry.com

www.ingramcontent.com/pod-product-compliance
Lightning Source LLC
Chambersburg PA
CBHW030311100526
44590CB00012B/592